Visions from
Stony Creek

Photos, poems and essays
of a place where a clear bubbling stream sings,
ancient oaks whisper secrets, and the lush green lowland reaches
a peeping crescendo on warm April nights—
where prairie grows,
the deer roam, and sandhill cranes raise their young.

Richard V. Finch

Published by Millin & Co
West Bend, Wisconsin 53095

Some contents of this book were previously published in "Along Stony Creek," and some of the poems were used by :
Algonquin Group of the Sierra Club
Land Conservation Partnership of Washington County
Outdoor Wisconsin, Wisconsin Public TV
Ozaukee Washington Land Trust
Washington County Land Conservation Department

Layout & Book Design: Susan Finch Millin   June Prairie Photo: Kathryn Leung   Time Capsule Photo: Chris Leung

Published by Millin & Co
1303 Timberline Drive, Suite 103, West Bend, WI 53095
millinco@sbcglobal.net
ISBN: 0-9761255-0-1
Printed in the United States of America

Preface

Not long ago, I was told in jest by a friend that when men grow old, they turn to poetry. It brought a chuckle, but so it was a few years ago when without real explanation, I began writing poems — first an attempt out of the blue on the back of an envelope, and later, after attending a writers workshop in Door County, many more and a few short essays. Most were about the natural world that surrounds our home here in Washington County, Wisconsin. Some adopted political themes, others were written for our young granddaughter in a humorous light, and a number touched on, well, what might be in the mind of an old man. When a few of the poems were used in the publications of environmental organizations, and one appeared on a Public TV program, I decided to publish "Along Stony Creek," a booklet of poems and essays reflecting a year's observations from out our kitchen window, and my walks in the field, woods and along the creek.

Then Lois presented me with a high-zoom digital camera for Christmas, and I could capture wildlife and scenery in great detail. Snapping photos soon became an obsession. Pictures are worth a thousand words, right? Finally, I came upon the idea of combining the pictures and writing — photo and poem, photo and haiku, photo and essay, picture and a few words.

Lois and Dick Finch

"Visions from Stony Creek" presents the image and soul of these fifty-seven acres of swamp, oak/hickory woods and open prairie. Its diversity is amazing if you consider the rapid development which typifies this area. We feel comfort that this place will be protected in perpetuity by an arrangement with the Ozaukee Washington Land Trust, and hope you will enjoy the peace and insight its "visions" can provide.

Richard V. Finch
October, 2004

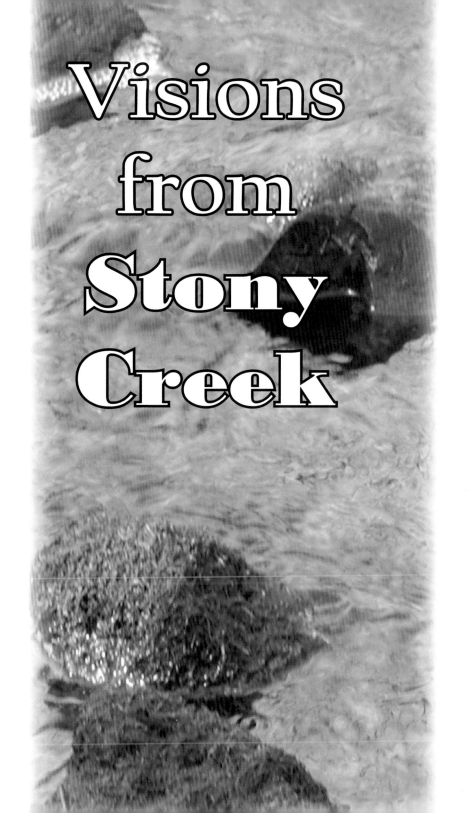

Visions from Stony Creek

Free

The last crystal of winter's snow,
turned free, quickly flows
down the slope to the lowland
where red skunk cabbage grows.

There, from atop the fuzzy willow
at the end of its short stay
a farewell from noisy red-wings
sends the droplet on its way.

Now onward the escapee,
joined by others on the run,
seeking creeks and rivers,
and praising the April sun.

Stony Creek

Stream bubbling through the lowland,
meandering under tamarack and ash,
giant boulders dumped by summer ice
haphazardly strewn in your path.

Cold clear waters ever singing
songs written at your beginning.
Oh, the stories you could chant,
tales of the bold, tales of fright,
of ancient ones red, and pioneers white.

Hide clad braves slowly wading,
spearing spring pike, upstream probing.

Farm children in straw hats,
with willow poles and catgut line,
catching square tailed trout, anytime.

The Great Spirit knows you hold more,
memories bright, deeds of gore:
of young love,
of thoughtless guns,
of drunken bullies,
of a young fawn's fun.

We treasure so much your ancient ballads,
be it resolved to preserve your domain,
so that forever others may relish
the intriguing, mysterious Stony Creek refrain.

Along a Path

Come sit down
along the swamp path.
Listen to the peeping frogs,
a red-wing serenade,
the mallard's invitation.
Smell the budding trees.
Smile at the rebirth
of cowslips,
skunk cabbage
and yellowing willow!

A s a young boy, I picked a trillium more
beautiful than this for my grandmother.
I can still see her smile as she placed it in a water
glass from the summer kitchen's open shelf — and
hear grandpa's warning that picking trilliums
was wrong. But there was a twinkle in his eye.

Pioneers

From a winter brush fire's black remains,
a pioneer settlement.
Fallen branches, orchard prunings,
and a brown-needled Christmas spruce,
now a colony of mushrooms,
a platoon of green sentinels.

Swamp Dance

A giant of lowland's edge,
put down by a flash
in a summer night's storm,
dances in dead spring grass
with barren limbs
that reach longingly
for the sky.

Temptress

Radiant, blooming white,

her fragrance overwhelms.

Bees from a country section

are drawn to her prairie island

to fulfill their mission.

The wild plum

reaches out

and guides you

to its tempting fruit.

"Nibble me, nibble me"

she whispers—

you yield

to the bittersweet promise.

Some creatures
are blessed with obscurity.

Morels scatter down the short wooded slope to the swamp— enough for tomorrow's breakfast.

June Prairie Stage

A hundred shades of green
rising from the earth,
blade after blade,
dancing in the sun.

They'll form a grand stage
for you and I to see —
it will be a short walk,
admission is free.

The play will be colorful,
ingenious, awesome —
the author great,
beyond comparison.

Oddball

Purple coneflowers in the field,
twenty thousand blooms a year.
And this summer, one plant is white
flowered.
What are the purples saying
as they gossip at their gatherings?
The oddball must have strange ways
like all elitist wackos,
liberal fools, fruitcakes.
Go back to where you came from,
or paint yourself purple
and hunker below the goldenrod.

Orange as the orange, cut in half on a nail,

eating sweet juicy pulp on a fence of split rails.

It carefully inspects
while whirling in place,
then warily probes
and partakes with delicate grace.

Wild brown-eyed susan
A bright and colorful friend
Her radiance blooms

Wetland Beauty

Put on your high boots, canvas hat and
a long-sleeved shirt—
discover the beauty of the wetland.

Jerusalem Artichoke

At the west end of this meandering ridge is an old wood duck nesting box mounted to a cedar post. I placed it there a decade ago, along a walking path overlooking the swamp. To my knowledge, it never sheltered a duck, but bluebirds, swallows and, yes, house sparrows and starlings have used it.

A while ago, the tall grass surrounding the box was mowed in a circular pattern to provide a feeding area for bluebirds. Freed of the thick growth, a bird-shaped mound of earth emerged before me — an ancient effigy mound, I speculated. To check my supposition, I talked to a daughter of the farmer who pastured cows on the ridge a half century ago. She recalled no such mound, but remembered the farm trash site was located on the west end of the field. Now covered and grown over, it probably was my discovery. But I decided the mound would remain, in my mind, a mystery— very possibly a bird effigy mound located on an old Indian campsite surrounded by superb hunting grounds.

Today, the walking path is rerouted a good distance to the north, and as a result, the site has been neglected. The grass has grown tall, and the box's clean-out door, ripped off by a predator, is a hazard to occupants. But yesterday, swaying yellow flowers reaching to the box caught my eye, and I plowed through the brome for a closer look. A woodchuck had dug a den near the post, and a clump of unusual sunflowers were rooted into the bared earth. Reference books have helped identify the brilliant flowering plant — Jerusalem Artichoke. Its scientific name, "Helianthus Tuberosus," recognizes a history of being raised by American Indians for the edible tuberous root. It remains in Wisconsin, especially near old native settlements.

How did artichoke seed get to the base of the nesting box? Blown by the wind, dropped by a bird, or ... there for a long, long time, waiting to be excavated from the fenced garden plot behind the deerhide and bark shelter of the Menomonee camp — right there, just beyond the earthen bird mound.

Welcome to a place where
wild grass and flowers grow,
deer and turky run free,
and circling hawks
like what they see below.

Sturgeon Spirit

This morning, a sturgeon
swam in the southern sky.
Its gigantic tail
propelled a mile-long body
east to west,
a sun-darkening shadow
forging a swift clear current.

I wondered how often
the sturgeon has emerged from a storm.
Perhaps rarely, and then only for old men
with worn eyes, but keen sight.

Prairie Bloom Creatures

The prairie's bloom attracts creatures
from Mexican rain forests,
the hollow tree along the creek,
miniature caverns in the prairie soil.

Some are blessed with magnificent wings,
others have organized social structures,
all have been assigned an important task.

Wild Apple

One late summer day
I went after invasive buckthorn,
with lopping shears and herbicide,
along the south slope
under slippery elm and white ash
where birds drop the seed.

On the far west end,
near a maple rising high above the swamp,
in a clump of young growth,
was a struggling wild apple tree.

A few apples clung to the tree,
and I picked the single red fruit
from the lowest branch—
it was tart, with a hint of sweetness,
the most delicious apple of my life.

Though armed with strong argument

the balanced centrist

in a dull "black or white" world

walks the path alone.

september

the final gasps of summer glory,
it's september, and it's sad
the long grasses are dull and browning,
coneflowers are limp and bowing,
all of nature is moving fast,
the big harvest is here at last,
you can sense the net
being cast

Red Cedars

Some label the red cedar
an aggressive weed tree,
best cut or burned
to keep the grasslands free.

But we admire it for what it provides,
a place for cardinals and finches
to nest and hide,
tasty berries for waxwings in fall,
and in the cold long winters,
it stands thick and tall.

Red cedars
have a place on our land,
here they will long remain.
We'd miss them, as would the birds,
standing sentinel
over their prairie domain.

Emerald River

In late summer, the prairie path was widened to
provide a fire break for an anticipated spring burn.
It soon became an emerald river embracing a golden sea.

Posts

We've got twenty-six posts on this place. Twenty-three are pressure treated young posts supporting bluebird houses with yellow numbers. We visit these posts every week or ten days to check the houses and the birds, to see if everything's okay.

The other three posts are of cedar, really more pole than post. We cut them "Up North" and brought them back. Cross pieces are mounted to the top to allow easy perching by large birds. These "raptor poles" stand high; they dominate, they rule. They attract the big ones — and our attention.

Not included in our post count, of course, are the old retired posts — the gray, abandoned fence posts which accomplished their jobs forty years ago when this was a dairy farm. About half the old posts no longer stand, and the wire that connected them is rusted ... brittle ... and broken.

October Harvest

Red-green apples,
some wormy scrubs,
some perfect as those
in a spring catalogue,
picked on a crisp sunny day
of my sixty-ninth October.

The shriveled, the bruised,
were thrown into high grass,
the undersized, partly wormy
pared and mashed
for pies and sauce,
the big, nearly flawless,
polished and displayed
in a walnut bowl
on the kitchen table.

Apples and life's memories,
a bushel of each,
have a lot in common.

Autumn Red

The old iceman
now prowls by night,
touching all in his path.
Most victims turn yellow,
bow, and die.
A few flush red in anger,
and resist.

In the late autumn
when bare branches frame the moon
cold nights warm the soul

Grandpa Oak

He's getting old
at a hundred-fifty years,
his limbs are brittle,
he's got shrinking feet.
The young and aggressive
are crowding him out,
but squirrels still
crawl up his back
for acorn treats.

We can see a few operating farms, but many have yielded to the bulldozer's blade. One wonders of our direction.

Wisconsin Earth

Wisconsin earth for sale

Rolling pristine woodland,

native campsite,

pioneer's dream.

Wisconsin earth for sale

Art and Edna's farm,

a hundred-sixty acres

mostly cleared and productive

with some wooded pasture,

house and barn electrified.

Wisconsin earth for sale

Offered by Willis & Wampus,

scenic ten acre farmette

with vintage home and outbuildings.

Also 150 prime acres

fifteen minutes northwest of town.

Wisconsin earth for sale

Heavenly Homes, Division of Patriot Reality

will build your dream home.

Gorgeous building sites, some wooded,

in exciting Farm Meadow Estates.

Full acre sites minutes from town,

low taxes, conventional septic, outstanding sunsets.

Wanted, Wisconsin earth

Urgent need for undeveloped acreage

in old agricultural belt.

US Department of Agriculture

Office of Food Scarcity

Be a responsible American, call today!

Old Frank

Oak and hickory leaves
are good storytellers
along November's wooded path.
Patches of pawed earth,
tree to tree runways,
whitewash splotches under the
roosting tree,
all whispered secrets.

Now under the big oak,
something else catches my eye —
uncovered by last night's wind,
an old twelve gauge shell,
corroded, faded red,
maybe fired fifty Novembers ago
when Old Frank
farmed this place.

I see a gray wrinkled man
sitting against the tree,
a single shot Winchester
cradled to his barn coat.
He glances down to
a pile of squirrels,
tips his green plaid hat,
and smiles.

They kick their heels
over the early winter field,
waving white flags,
playing deer tag.

Thanksgiving Turkeys

Turkeys in the prairie,
now a stone's throw away,
bring smiles to our Thanksgiving
table
as we confront their distant cousin,
red cranberries,
pear-lime jello,
mashed potatoes,
golden corn,
and pumpkin pie.

The menu was the same
twelve years ago
when wild turkeys last visited
on Thanksgiving day.
There were three more chairs
at the table then,
one belonged to Grandpa John
who spotted the turkeys
high in a big swamp oak.

Last Deer Hunt

In the bleak November dusk,
chilly and damp, I shiver and groan.
Westerly driving freezing gusts
penetrate the marrow of my old bones.

Cold as sitting on a subzero rock,
huddled in a blind surrounded by brush,
hand clasped to the muzzleloader stock,
I await my last white-tailed buck.

Stiff and numb, body and mind,
reactions slow, thinking a grind,
I'm half asleep, it seems a dream,
on a day like this, few deer are seen.

But now a big buck is staring at me.
Is it an antlered illusion I perceive?
For five minutes, we're eye to eye,
he then decides I pose no threat,
and with rifle uncocked, I nod goodbye,
my last chance, and I have no regret!

Front Porch Enemy

It was early one morn, at the time of ripe corn,
when we first heard the noise on our porch.
At first a faint peck, peck, pecking
like a watch ticking —
our slumber seemed reinforced.

Then as the sun was warming,
the noise became alarming —
grumbling, I stumbled to look.
And saw a feathered fiend attacking,
drilling, chiseling and banging,
the hollow posts supporting the roof.

Black and white his body, his red spotted head a'flailing,
to gain access to the chamber inside,
but finding a treated interior, to trees quite inferior,
he retreated to the wooded hillside.

After patching and sanding, matching and staining
we thought our bird problem done.
But then without warning, he was back to his boring,
by the first light of the winter sun.

He's now back each rotten morning
with his maddening rapping —
we've had great trouble sleeping,
and yes, even napping.

It's not to our liking, this lack of sleeping,
and we scheme to rid ourselves of this foe.
Three wind chimes are ringing and clanging,
and for added repelling,
five foam owls are staring —
be there more, we implore, let us know !

Five Friends

The guys are lined up
on the rail
discussing the important issues:
the weather,
the food supply,
how to avoid hawks, fox, and
weapons of mass destruction
in the hands of evil men.

Christmas Rainbow

The snow melted
and there came a sign —
a rare December rainbow
reaching from the east horizon,
touching on the bold grasses,
and settling into the tamarack.
The Indian, Switch and Blue Stem
stretched, long and yellow, in praise,
the mighty Red Oak bowed,
and a circling Red-tail
spread its light-gray wings.

Old Man Cold

in from the Canadian wilds
a man ugly, old
with long clear brittle fingers
and toeless stump feet, cold

ancient as the world
his gray wrinkled face, mean
with pale white cheeks a'blowing
a heartless freezing breeze

spreading chill and stiffness
on fields and quaint towns
with a harsh cloak of white
and an eerie howling sound

standing in his presence
puts shivers up the spine
and listening to him
all too often
turns rosy ears to white

this winter started mild
we thought he had died
but today "Old Man Cold"
came back,
he came back quite alive

Ringo

In our first eleven years here, we occasionally heard the crow of a pheasant rooster, but never actually saw one. Then early one winter morning, a beautiful ring-neck appeared in our backyard, and subsequently each morning, to perform a peculiar routine. At dawn he would rap at his reflection on the cellar window, then feed on sunflower seeds that had fallen from the bird feeder. We started to put out sunflower heads to supplement his sporadic food source and eventually he learned to fly up to the platform feeder for easy feasting. We soon considered him a family member, naming him "Ringo."

As winter wore on, Ringo's health seemed to be going downhill, and he adopted a bowed posture as if in prayer. Then he disappeared.

The next fall, we were delighted to host another ring-neck. He was even more colorful than Ringo, and though not nearly as friendly, we named him "Ringo II." He stayed for over six months, often perching on the backyard split-rail fence.

It's been a couple of years since Ringo II; but on snowy mornings, we sometimes catch ourselves glancing out the back window looking for him — or perhaps Ringo III, exploring the winter home of his ancestors.

Bear

For a hundred centuries
the black bear ruled the creek.
Now its ghost
emerges thru the ice,
etching a whimsical reminder
of bygone times.

Winter Morning Sampler

Turkeys scavenged acorns in the early morning woods, and they must have had quite a party. Their scattered scratches through the snow spur an aging memory of snitched icing on my granddaughter's second birthday cake. The disturbed areas under the oaks are joined by striding three-toed tracks that eventually head to the creek where they disperse into the lowland.

The cold snap has sealed the creek, even silenced the rapids. The clear rippling flow is now a paved highway for rabbits and coyotes, and the bridge is an overpass. Rabbits use the bridge, but the coyotes, never — even when in pursuit.

Deer tracks lead out to the prairie, then up the path to the orchard where skeleton branches tenaciously grasp a few shriveled apples. Any apples within reaching distance of an outstretched deer have long been harvested, and those that now fall are relished by the deer and rabbits each evening.

The deer tracks meander east, out of the apple trees. I follow them to the driveway, then veer off for the house. In the garage, I find a freshly filled suet log Lois left on the galvanized trash can lid. That's her instruction for me to feed the birds. I hang the log from a shepherd's hook in the backyard prairie, then go inside to watch the chickadees, woodpeckers and juncos from the kitchen window.

Conifer Conference

The conifers of Stony Creek responded to the notice enthusiastically. A conference to address the growing danger of man was long overdue. The oldest and wisest, a Red Cedar on the south bluff, was unanimously elected chairman and it called the gathering to order. After some thought, the Cedar proposed a set of ground rules — each tree would be given three minutes to address the assembly, then the chairman would finalize and establish a battle plan. The Pines, Firs, and Spruces all voiced approval— even the Tamaracks, in the midst of dormancy, managed a nod.

A Scotch Pine from atop the slope spoke first, "They're Anglo-elitists," it said, "Did you know most of my family is from mainland Europe and the fringes of Asia?" Then it became emotional and accused humans of uprooting family members, cramming them on deplorable sailing ships, and transplanting them throughout the world to serve as slaves. It suggested all trees in the world go on a hunger strike, thus depriving man of his needed lumber. "That'll shake 'em into reality," it stammered.

The Colorado Spruce from the ridge jumped in: "Don't think it's only you immigrants," it said, "Like all my family is from Colorado? And look what they've done to my kind — dragging us to the dirty cities of the east to spruce up their development. We don't belong there, and it degrades our heritage. I'd suggest we just stop throwing off oxygen, but I'm not sure how we'd do it." Then it added, "Or maybe we Colorados could secretly pollinate with off-color mates to give them ugly landscaping — that's something to ponder."

The Firs, Red Pines, and White Pines followed with additional tales of exploitation, and some offered similar remedies. A White Cedar suggested that humans had thoughtlessly exterminated many predator animals, and browsing deer had become so numerous that young White Cedar were a rarity. It believed the Great Spirit Tree had answered prayers regarding both man and deer by sending a strange disease that effected their brains. It pleaded for a tree-wide prayer campaign.

An old Tamarack, barely able to speak, complained of the draining and filling of swamps, and it offered to chair a committee to motivate Tamaracks to refrain from growing new needles for two full years.

Finally. after soliciting further input, Chairman Cedar began its closing comments: "My family is native to about 40 of the states established by the enemy," it said with an angry shake of lower limbs. "We've been cut, burned, and buried by humans for 500 years. Now they've developed herbicide, acid rain and global warming to complete the genocide of Red Cedar—all Cedar— all conifers! Friends, they will not be stopped, and we must adopt a long range pragmatic approach. I submit we immediately begin to secure our finest seed in hiding places throughout our range. Then, in perhaps a half-century, long after we've all been done in, our descendants will inherit the earth. If I recall my ecology lessons, our death is their death—the humans will soon die out. Yes, our seed will arise in a cleansed human-free environment, and we will have the world." And at that, the conifers bid each other farewell and prepared to hide their seed.

Chickadee Buddy

My friendly winged buddy
is tiny with a black cap —
he has perched on my shoulder
and once, even my hat!

But he never stays long,
then he's off feeding on seeds
and little round grubs
from the goldenrod weeds.

And when the snow comes down
and Christmas approaches,
he becomes a living ornament
in the green backyard spruces.

Winter Nests

Cold and lonely,
the winter nests,
their young fledged,
the season passed.
Memories
sustain them.

Smiling is the crow

which oversees unspoiled fields

It sees tomorrow

Long Winter

How long will winter last ?
Beyond the wild geranium,
the coneflowers,
the asters?
Two hundred lifetimes ago,
shadows on white ice
danced through the summer.
Might the Great Spirit
again write a final chapter
and begin a new book?

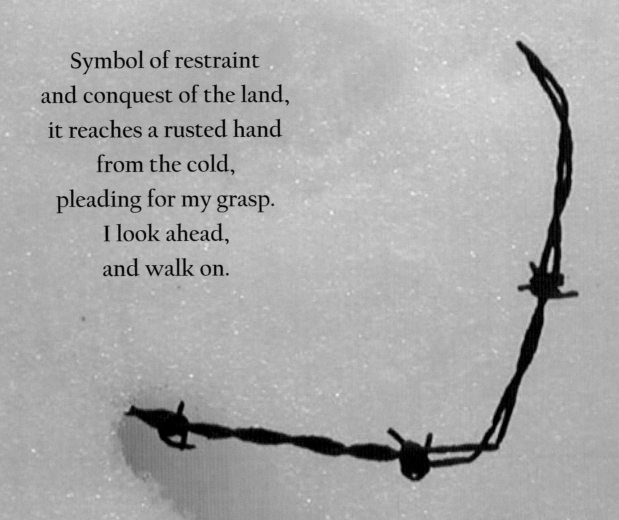

Symbol of restraint
and conquest of the land,
it reaches a rusted hand
from the cold,
pleading for my grasp.
I look ahead,
and walk on.

Winter woods diary,
the final page.
How soon the trilliums?